Newcastle Lions

THE WORLD'S SMARTEST ANIMALS

DOLPHINS

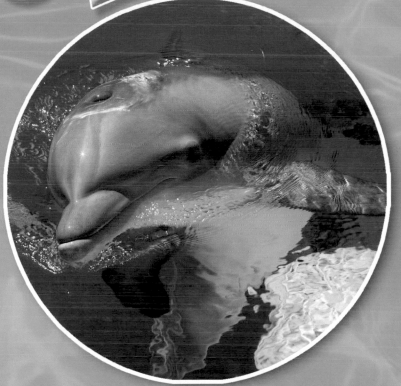

by Ruth Owen

WINDMILL
BOOKS

New York

Published in 2012 by Windmill Books, An Imprint of Rosen Publishing
29 East 21st Street, New York, NY 10010

Editor for Ruby Tuesday Books Ltd: Mark J. Sachner
U.S. Editor: Sara Antill
Designer: Emma Randall
Consultant: Dr. David Lusseau, Lecturer in marine populations, University of Aberdeen, Institute of Biological and Environmental Sciences

Photo Credits: Cover, 1, 5, 6, 7 (center left), 7 (bottom), 8–9, 19, 21, 22–23, 24 (center), 28–29 © Shutterstock; 7 (center right), 10–11, 13, 15, 16–17, 24–25 (main) © FLPA; 27 © U.S. Navy (public domain).

Library of Congress Cataloging-in-Publication Data

Owen, Ruth, 1967–
 Dolphins / By Ruth Owen.
     p. cm. — (The world's smartest animals)
 Includes index.
 ISBN 978-1-61533-379-0 (library binding) — ISBN 978-1-61533-416-2 (pbk.) —
 ISBN 978-1-61533-476-6 (6-pack)
 1. Dolphins—Juvenile literature. I. Title.
 QL737.C432O944 2012
 599.53—dc22

                          2011013474

Manufactured in the United States of America

CPSIA Compliance Information: Batch #RTS1102WM: For Further Information contact Windmill Books, New York, New York at 1-866-478-0556

CONTENTS

OCEAN HEROES

Several people are having fun swimming in the ocean.
Suddenly, one of the swimmers spots a great white shark.
They are in great danger!
Just then, seven rescuers speed toward the swimmers.
The brave rescuers circle the swimmers.
For 40 minutes, they keep the shark away
until a rescue boat arrives.

This amazing event happened in New Zealand in 2004.
The swimmers weren't protected by a team of brave lifeguards,
however. Their rescuers were seven bottlenose dolphins!
The dolphins seemed to understand that the swimmers
needed help.

Scientists still have a lot to learn about dolphins, but they
know dolphins can **communicate** with each other.
Dolphins can teach each other new things and even
solve problems. Scientists also know that these
helpful ocean heroes are very smart!

DOLPHIN SKILLS

Some dolphins can even do math! At the Dolphin Research Center in Florida, dolphins were trained to do a numbers test. They were shown pairs of blackboards with white dots on them. The dolphins had to choose the board with the fewest dots. Some dolphins answered correctly 80 percent of the time.

Two dolphins leap from the water as they chase behind a boat!

ALL ABOUT DOLPHINS

Dolphins belong to an animal group called cetaceans. This group includes whales, dolphins, and porpoises. All cetaceans are mammals.

Cetaceans are divided into baleen whales and toothed whales. Baleen whales are animals such as blue whales and gray whales. These animals feed by swallowing big mouthfuls of water. Then they filter tiny ocean creatures out of the water using body parts called baleen plates. The toothed whales group includes animals such as dolphins, orcas, porpoises, and sperm whales. These animals are hunters. They grab their **prey** using their teeth.

There are many different types of dolphins. Some dolphins live in the ocean. Others live in rivers. The best-known type of dolphin is the smiley-faced bottlenose dolphin!

Dorsal fin for balance

Blowhole

Tail flukes for power

Flipper for steering

Like all mammals, cetaceans have to breathe air. They breathe by opening and closing a blowhole on top of their heads. They have to swim up to the water's surface to breathe.

Orcas are actually a type of dolphin.

A pair of Amazon River dolphins

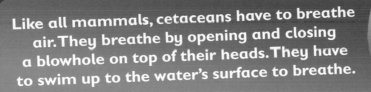

A bottlenose dolphin

LiFE iN A SCHOOL

Dolphins live in groups called schools. A school might contain just two dolphins or it may have thousands of members.

During the day, a school may split up into several smaller groups. It might also join other schools to form a bigger group. Sometimes female dolphins form a nursery school so that they can help each other look after their babies, or calves.

Living in a school is one way to protect against **predators**. If a predator, such as a shark, tries to attack a single dolphin, it is less likely to be eaten if many other dolphins are around. Dolphins may defend themselves by hitting a predator with their snout or tail. They can also swim away fast. Bottlenose dolphins can reach speeds of up to 18 miles an hour (29 km/h).

A school of dolphins

Sometimes dolphins make leaps and other movements perfectly timed with each other. This could be a sign to predators or other dolphins that they are a strong team. Sometimes a dolphin will swim with its flipper resting on another dolphin's back. This may be a sign that they are friends.

DOLPHIN SKILLS

DOLPHIN TALK

Dolphins communicate with each other using sounds and movements.

Dolphin talk includes grunts, moans, and high-pitched chirps and whistles. Scientists are trying to learn if each dolphin has its own special whistle, known as a signature whistle. They think dolphins might be able to recognize each other by their signature whistles. This would be like you recognizing your best friend's voice if she or he shouted to you in a crowd.

Sometimes dolphins leap into the air as high as 20 feet (6 m). They then splash back into the water on their sides or backs. This is called **breaching**. Scientists think it could be a way of sending messages, such as "let's go!"

Leaping and breaching could be play or a way of sending messages.

DOLPHIN SKILLS

A dolphin will hit the water with its tail or its whole body. This makes a loud, booming noise. The noise doesn't travel very far in water, though. Dolphins can use this noise to communicate with their school without other dolphins being able to hear them.

SEEING WITH SOUND

Dolphins hunt for fish. They also eat squid and sometimes shrimp. They grab their prey with their teeth. They then swallow it whole without chewing.

It's hard to see very far underwater, so dolphins use a way of finding prey called **echolocation**. A dolphin sends out clicking sounds into the water. When the sounds hit something, such as a fish, they bounce back to the dolphin as echoes. The echoes tell the dolphin how far away the fish is, its size, its shape, and even its speed.

Dolphins send out the sounds from the rounded, fatty part of their foreheads. This is called the melon. They pick up the echoes through their lower jaws.

Dolphins use echolocation to build a picture of their underwater world!

Dolphins living in the ocean are surrounded by water, but they live like desert animals! They cannot drink the seawater because it is too salty. They get the water they need from their food. Their bodies are also designed to use as little water as possible.

DOLPHIN SKILLS

Melon

A dolphin hunting bigeye scad fish

DOLPHIN TEAM WORK

Dolphins know that the smartest way to catch a big meal is by using teamwork!

When dolphins find a school of fish, some of the dolphins will start to circle the fish. The dolphins swim in smaller and smaller circles. This forces the fish into a tight ball. Then, the dolphins can dive into the ball of fish and easily grab a meal.

On the coast of Laguna, in Brazil, dolphins and the local fishermen have worked as a team for over 150 years. The fishermen wait in the shallow water with their fishing nets. The dolphins drive fish toward them. At just the right moment, the dolphins dive out of the water. This is the signal to the fishermen to throw their nets. The fishermen catch lots of fish, and the dolphins snap up any fish that escape!

DOLPHIN SKILLS

On the South Carolina coast, dolphins sometimes drive schools of fish toward the shore. The dolphins then swim fast toward the shore. This creates a big wave. The wave washes the fish and the dolphins onto the beach. The dolphins grab as many fish as they can and then slide back into the water!

14

Dolphins circling a ball of small fish

MOTHERS AND BABIES

Dolphins give birth to one calf at a time. A mother dolphin will care for her calf for between two and five years.

Dolphins are born underwater. They are normally born tail first. As soon as the calf's head leaves the mother's body, the calf must start to breathe air or it will drown. The mother pushes the calf to the water's surface so it can breathe.

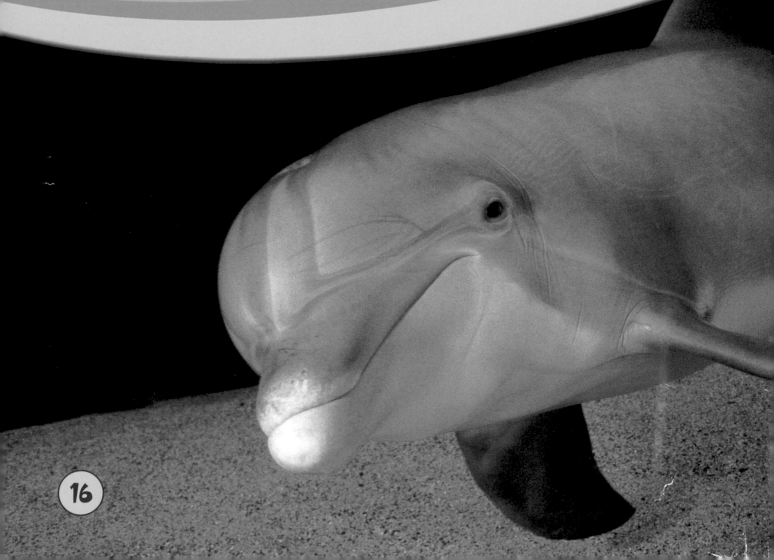

A dolphin learns many of the things it needs to know from its mother and other dolphins. The calf will learn how to use echolocation and catch prey. It will also learn how to dive, breach, and communicate with other dolphins.

A young calf will get help from its mother to move along. It stays close to her body, and because it is small, it gets pulled through the water in her **slipstream**.

A bottlenose dolphin calf and its mother

When a mother dolphin needs to look for food, she will get another female to babysit her calf. She might leave her calf with its grandmother or an older sister.

DOLPHIN SKILLS

OUR FRIEND THE DOLPHIN

When people get into trouble in the ocean, dolphins sometimes help them.

Surfer Todd Endris was attacked by a great white shark while surfing off Monterey, California. The shark badly injured his back and right leg. A school of dolphins surrounded Todd. They kept the shark away and allowed Todd to catch a wave and make it back to the beach.

Filippo the dolphin was well known for playing with swimmers off the coast of Manfredonia, Italy. One day, 14-year-old Davide Ceci fell from his father's boat. David could not swim, and at first his father did not realize he had fallen. Filippo appeared and pushed the drowning boy back to the boat so his father could grab him.

Dolphins sometimes help other animals. Two pygmy sperm whales were stuck in shallow water on Mahia Beach in New Zealand. Human rescuers had not been able to get them back out to sea. Then, Moko, a local dolphin, arrived. The scared whales calmed down and let Moko lead them back out into the ocean!

DOLPHIN SKILLS

Dolphins often swim close to divers and swimmers.

SO HOW SMART ARE DOLPHINS?

A bottlenose dolphin named Akeakamai was trained to answer questions. She could even solve problems!

Akeakamai's trainer asked her questions using hand signals. She had to answer by pressing a "yes" or "no" paddle on the side of the pool.

The trainer might throw a pipe and a basket into the pool. If Akeakamai was asked, "Is there a pipe?" She would answer yes. If she was asked, "Is there a surfboard?" she would answer no. This showed she was smart enough to remember a surfboard and the sign for surfboard, even though there wasn't one in her pool.

Sometimes the question was trickier. One time a pipe and basket were thrown into the pool. The trainer then asked Akeakamai to collect a hoop and put it in the basket. There was no hoop in the water. So, she solved the tricky problem by collecting the basket, taking it to the paddles, and pressing no!

DOLPHIN SKILLS

Most animals don't recognize their own face in a mirror. Dolphins, however, understand they are seeing their own reflection. Some dolphins had black marks put on their bodies in places they couldn't see, such as near their dorsal fin. The dolphins used mirrors in their tank to check out the marks!

Smart dolphins know that signs can stand for an object such as a hoop.

DOLPHIN ORIGINALS

People in different places have different customs and ways of doing things. Over many years, everyone in that place learns its customs and activities. We call this culture.

Some scientists believe that dolphins in different areas have their own culture, too!

In Adelaide, Australia, wild dolphins have been seen tail-walking. Wild dolphins hardly ever tail-walk. Scientists believe the wild dolphins learned to tail-walk from a dolphin named Billie.

In the 1980s, Billie became trapped in a marina, a place for keeping boats. For three weeks, Billie was kept in a **dolphinarium** before she went back to the ocean. The dolphins at the dolphinarium were trained to perform in shows. Billie saw the performing dolphins tail-walking and taught herself the trick. She has now passed the trick on to other dolphins where she lives.

Sponges are ocean animals.

Dolphins in Shark Bay, in western Australia, put protective sponges on their snouts when they are looking for food on the seabed. This is not something that other dolphins do. Scientists believe that a dolphin in the area invented this activity, and now others have learned to do it.

DOLPHIN SKILLS

22

A bottlenose dolphin tail-walking

PERFORMING DOLPHINS

Dolphins can be trained to do tricks. People sometimes capture them from the ocean and train them to perfom in dolphinarium shows.

Not everyone agrees with this. Some people feel it isn't right to make wild animals do tricks and keep them in small tanks of water. A bottlenose dolphin that lives in the ocean might swim 40 miles (64 km) in a day. In a tank or pool, it can only swim for a few seconds before reaching

This dolphin can only swim in circles in this small, bare tank.

These dolphins are training in an ocean pen at a research center.

a wall. These dolphins cannot use all of their natural skills. Dolphins hunt for live prey as a team, but captive dolphins rely on people to feed them.

Today, some **research centers** combine studying dolphins with entertainment. These centers try to give the dolphins a more natural life. The dolphins live in large, open-air pens that are in the ocean. Scientists and trainers work with the dolphins to find out more about them. Visitors can see the dolphins in action and learn what people should do to protect them and their ocean home.

DOLPHINS IN THE MILITARY

The U.S. Navy trains bottlenose dolphins to help find underwater mines. These explosive devices may be used during wars to blow up ships.

It is difficult to find mines deep on the seabed. Dolphins can dive to great depths and use echolocation to find mines. When a dolphin finds a mine, it places a marker near it with a **buoy** that floats to the surface. The dolphin then leaves the area, and a navy team can remove or explode the mine.

The U.S. Navy says that the dolphins are not in danger because they cannot set off the mines. They say the dolphins' work saves lives, but some people feel that animals should not be used to help humans in this way. What do you think?

Bottlenose dolphins can hold their breath for up to 20 minutes. They can dive to depths below 600 feet (183 m).

Dolphin Skills

This U.S. Navy dolphin is wearing a "pinger" so its trainer can keep track of it.

27

A FUTURE WITH DOLPHINS

Unfortunately, people can make it hard for dolphins to survive. Some types of dolphins are now endangered.

Every year, thousands of dolphins are trapped underwater in fishing nets and drown. **Conservation groups** are working with the fishing industry to find ways to catch fish without also catching dolphins. They also encourage people to only buy seafood that is marked "dolphin friendly."

In some areas, people are catching so many fish that there are not enough fish left for the dolphins to eat!

Dolphins can be harmed by pollution, such as oil that spills from ships or drilling equipment. **Sewage** and poisonous chemicals are also dumped in rivers and oceans.

Dolphins cannot survive without fish to eat and clean, safe water. People must work hard to protect dolphins and their **habitat**.

Dolphins rely on sound and echolocation to communicate, find prey, and avoid predators. Today, the ocean is filled with noise from ships, pleasure boats, and oil and gas drilling. Scientists are very worried that this human-made noise may be harmful to dolphins and other ocean animals.

DOLPHIN SKILLS

GLOSSARY

breaching (BREECH-ing)
When an ocean animal, such as a dolphin, whale, or shark, leaps out of the sea and then crashes back into the water on its side or back.

buoy (BOO-ee)
An object, such as a ball, that floats and is anchored in the water as a kind of marker.

cetacean (sih-TAY-shun)
A member of the cetacean group of animals, which is made up of whales, dolphins, and porpoises. These animals are mammals that live in water.

communicate (kuh-MYOO-nih-kayt)
To share facts or feelings.

conservation group
(kon-sur-VAY-shun GROOP)
An organization that does work to protect the natural world from damage by humans. The group might campaign to protect a habitat or a type of wild animal.

custom (KUST-tum)
Something that a particular group of people do regularly and have done for many years, such as celebrating a holiday or eating a special meal on a particular day.

dolphinarium (dol-fih-NAYR-ee-um)
A place where dolphins are kept in a pool, or in a pen in the ocean. The dolphins might be kept to be studied or to perform shows for visitors.

echolocation
(eh-koh-loh-KAY-shun)
One way that a dolphin collects information about its environment. A dolphin sends out sounds that bounce off objects such as fish, predators, and rocks. When the sounds, or echoes, travel back to the dolphin, it uses them to create a picture of things it cannot see with its eyes.

endangered (in-DAYN-jerd)
In danger of no longer existing.

habitat (HA-buh-tat)
The place where an animal or plant normally lives. A habitat may be a rain forest, the ocean, or a backyard.

mammal (MA-mul)
A warm-blooded animal that has a backbone and hair, breathes air, and feeds milk to its young.

mine (MYN)
An explosive device that can float in water or lie on the seabed. Some underwater mines explode if a ship hits them. Other types explode if they detect a ship passing overhead. Mines can also be buried on land to injure or kill people and destroy vehicles that touch them.

predator (PREH-duh-ter)
An animal that hunts and kills other animals for food.

prey (PRAY)
An animal that is hunted by another animal as food.

research center (REE-serch SEN-tur)
A place where scientists study something.

school (SKOOL)
A group of dolphins or fish.

sewage (SOO-ij)
Human waste.

slipstream (SLIP-streem)
The area behind a fast-moving object where a pulling effect is created that may drag other objects along.

WEB SITES

For Web resources related to the subject of this book, go to: www.windmillbooks.com/weblinks and select this book's title.

READ MORE

King, Zelda. *Dolphins*. Marine Mammals. New York: PowerKids Press, 2012.

Nicklin, Flip and Linda Nicklin. *Face to Face with Dolphins*. Des Moines, IA: National Geographic Children's Books, 2009.

Simon, Seymour. *Dolphins*. New York: HarperCollins Publishers, 2009.

INDEX